CARING FOR HERMITS CRAB

A handbook on how to care for your hermit crab

Guide to Happy and Healthy Hermit Crab training

Dr Ashley Ruell

Copyright © 2023 Dr Ashley Ruell

All Rights Reserved

Table of Contents

INTRODUCTION 6

CHAPTER 1 7

ESSENTIALS OF A HABITAT: CREATING THE IDEAL HOUSE FOR YOUR HERMIT CRAB 7

CHAPTER 2 15

NUTRITION & DIET: SUGGESTIONS FOR A HEALTHY HERMIT 15

CHAPTER 3 23

SELECTING THE CORRECT SHELLS: AN UNDERSTANDING OF THE PROCESS 23

CHAPTER 4 31

TEMPERATURE AND HUMIDITY: ESTABLISHING THE PERFECT SETTING 31

CHAPTER 5 .... **40**

TAKING CARE OF YOUR HERMIT CRAB AND GETTING ALONG WITH IT: APPROPRIATE WAYS TO 40

CHAPTER 6 .... **49**

HEALTH INDICATIONS: RECOGNIZING AND TREATING TYPICAL HERMIT CRAB PROBLEMS 49

CHAPTER 7 .... **59**

MOLTING MATTERS: HANDLING THE PROCESS OF MOLTING SAFELY 59

CHAPTER 8 .... **70**

SOCIAL DYNAMICS: PERSPECTIVES ON THE COMPANIONSHIP AND BEHAVIOR OF HERMIT CRABS .. 70

CHAPTER 9 .... **82**

Tank Upkeep: Maintaining a Scenic and Cozy Habitat 82

CHAPTER 10 98

Being Prepared for Unexpected Events: Emergency Preparedness 98

FAQS 111

Introduction

Greetings from the intriguing world of caring for hermit crabs! These fascinating crabs are unusual and interesting pets, but giving them a shell to live in isn't enough to ensure their wellbeing. We'll cover a wide range of important subjects in this guide, from creating the ideal habitat and providing a balanced meal to comprehending their molting process and creating a positive social environment. Join us as we explore the nuances of hermit crab care and maintenance for a satisfying and enlightening experience, whether you're an experienced hermit crab fan or a novice ready to start this fascinating adventure.

Chapter 1

Essentials of a Habitat: Creating the Ideal House for Your Hermit Crab

Making sure your hermit crab has the best possible home is essential to its longevity and general well-being. We'll go over every aspect of habitat necessities in this extensive guide, helping you to set up the ideal living space for your crustacean buddy.

1: Recognizing the Natural Environment
It's important to comprehend the natural habitat of hermit crabs before getting into the mechanics of building one. Tropical and subtropical areas are home to hermit crabs, which prefer warm, humid climates with access to both land and water. Maintaining these circumstances is essential for a hermit crab to be content and healthy.

2. Choosing the Appropriate Enclosure

The first step in building the perfect environment is selecting the appropriate enclosure. Choose a tank with adequate ventilation to keep the air flowing and avoid losing too much humidity. Make sure the aquarium is large enough to support the growth of your hermit crab, and it can be made of glass or plastic. Remember that hermit crabs are gregarious animals, so if you want to encourage a natural group dynamic, think about getting more than one.

3. Choosing the Substrate

To replicate its natural habitat, your hermit crab's substrate, or flooring, is essential. A good blend that offers burrow-friendly texture and moisture retention is made of sphagnum moss, sand, and coconut coir. To aid in burrowing and molting, make sure the substrate is at least three times the height of your largest crab.

4: Light and Heat

Keeping hermit crabs at the proper temperature is essential to their wellbeing. The ideal temperature range is 75–85°F (24–29°C), and to generate a warm area, use a heat source such as an under-tank heater. Moreover, full-spectrum lighting promotes natural behaviors and helps with vitamin D synthesis.

5: Regulation of Humidity

Hermit crabs prefer high humidity conditions, with a 70–80% range being ideal. This can be accomplished by providing a shallow dish of dechlorinated water for them to immerse in and daily misting the habitat. Make sure the water is just the right depth so your crabs can stay hydrated and maintain their proper moisture levels.

6: Areas of Land and Water

Providing both land and water regions is necessary to create a habitat that resembles the natural habitat. Add a deeper pool for soaking and a small dish with fresh water for sipping. Include decorations or pebbles to provide climbing chances that reflect the variety of terrain seen in their natural settings.

7: Outfitting the Encampment

Provide your hermit crab with a variety of hiding places and climbing structures to improve its surroundings. Add PVC pipes, driftwood, and coconut hides to provide them many options for hiding and exploring. Stress is decreased and natural activities are encouraged in a well-furnished setting.

8: Selecting Appropriate Shells

A hermit crab's shell is essential to its identity and serves as more than just a place to live. To enable your crab to select and switch out its shells as it grows, provide an assortment of shells in various sizes and forms. To avoid injuries, make sure the apertures are smooth and devoid of sharp edges.

9: Keeping Your Habitat Clean

It is essential to provide your hermit crab regular care. Spot clean the substrate, clean and replenish water dishes frequently, and remove any leftover food right away. To preserve hygiene, do a complete substrate replacement every few months.

10: Keeping an eye on health and behavior

Your hermit crab's behavior can provide you with insight into how healthy it is. Hermit crabs in good health are gregarious, energetic, and display typical climbing and exploring tendencies. Observe their feeding patterns and be on the lookout for any indications of stress or disease. See a veterinarian with experience treating exotic animals if you see any anomalies.

11: Offering a Well-Composed Diet

The foundation of caring for a hermit crab is a healthy diet. Provide a range of diets, such as commercial hermit crab pellets, fresh produce, calcium and protein sources, and fruits and vegetables. To support the health of their exoskeleton, give them access to a shallow dish of seawater and add cuttlebone to their diet.

12: Managing and Communicating

Hermit crabs can benefit from interaction even if they are not pets that love being handled frequently. By putting your hand in the environment and letting them come to you at their own pace, you may gently stimulate exploration. Always treat them gently and try not to get too worked up over them.

13: The Molting Procedure

Owners of hermit crabs must comprehend the molting process. Crabs are very fragile during their molting period, so it's important to provide them a calm, safe space. Make sure the humidity is at the right level and don't bother your crab during this time. Keep spare shells on hand in case the crabs change their shells after molting.

14. Social Dynamics

Hermit crabs are gregarious animals that do best in their own species' company. If you want to promote natural activities like grooming and shell swapping, think about keeping many crabs. Make sure there are enough hiding places in the environment to lessen the likelihood of disputes.

15: Being Ready for Emergencies

Part of owning a hermit crab responsibly is being ready for anything. Establish a special isolation tank for sick or injured crabs, and educate yourself on prevalent medical conditions. Become acquainted with an exotic pet veterinarian who can offer specialist care when required.

In conclusion, creating the ideal habitat for your hermit crab requires a careful balancing act between environmental elements, appropriate diet, and knowledge of their distinct behaviors. You may support the health and well-being of these intriguing crustaceans by devoting time and energy to establishing a stimulating habitat that allows them to exhibit their natural tendencies and prosper.

Chapter 2

Nutrition & Diet: Suggestions for a Healthy Hermit

For your hermit crab to remain healthy and vibrant, it is essential to provide a diet that is both balanced and nutrient-rich. We will cover every aspect of diet and nutrition in this extensive guide, along with feeding suggestions to ensure your hermit crab thrives in captivity.

1: Knowing the Dietary Requirements for Hermit Crabs

Hermit crabs are omnivores, which means they eat both vegetation and animals. They eat a wide range of things in the wild, such as algae, small insects, decomposing plants, and even carrion. For the sake of their general welfare, it is imperative to replicate this varied diet in captivity.

2. Commercial Pellets of Hermit Crab

Hermit crab pellets from commercial sources are a handy and well-balanced staple in their diet. Seek for premium pellets that have a combination of vitamins, minerals, and protein. Pellets are the cornerstone of their diet and can be provided every day to guarantee a steady supply of vital nutrients.

3. Just-picked fruits and veggies

To add more vitamins and minerals, serve a range of fresh fruits and vegetables. Popular fruit options include apples, bananas, and berries; for a well-rounded diet, consider veggies like carrots, spinach, and kale. Before giving these foods to your hermit crab, make sure they've been well-washed and are free of pesticides.

4: Sources of Protein

For hermit crabs to grow and undergo molting, protein is essential. Add foods high in protein to their diet, such as shellfish, modest portions of lean meat, and boiled eggs. Crab, shrimp, and fish flesh provide great options. You should not use oils for cooking or flavoring since they can damage your hermit crab.

5: Foods High in Calcium

For the exoskeleton of a hermit crab to remain healthy, calcium is essential. Provide calcium-rich materials like cuttlebone, broken eggshells, and real coral. These can be added to their meals or left in the environment. Making sure they are getting enough calcium is important, especially while they are molting and their exoskeleton is changing a lot.

6: Requirements for Hydration

Keeping well-hydrated is just as crucial as feeding a healthy diet. Make sure there is always a shallow dish of freshwater that has been dechlorinated available. Offer a dish of saltwater as well to aid with their osmoregulation. Your hermit crab should have easy access to both dishes so they may adjust their moisture content as needed.

7: Steer clear of toxic foods

Hermit crabs may be poisoned or harmed by some diets. Never give children dairy products, sugary sweets, processed or salty foods, or anything seasoned with seasonings or additives. Avoiding citrus fruits is also advised because their digestive systems may find them to be excessively acidic. Before introducing new foods, it is imperative to do your homework and be aware of any potential risks.

8: Feeding Timetable

Your hermit crab will have a steady and healthy diet if you establish a regular feeding plan. It is possible to give commercial pellets every day, but it is also possible to give fresh produce, fruits, and protein sources occasionally. Keep an eye on their eating patterns and modify the amounts to suit their needs and tastes.

9: Presentation of Food

Since hermit crabs are scavengers by nature, it can be beneficial to arrange their food in a way that promotes their natural scavenging habits. To replicate natural food sources, scatter food throughout the habitat and utilize shallow dishes. This encourages both physical and mental exercise, leading to a healthier and more active lifestyle.

10: Addendum

The basis of nutrition for hermit crabs is a well-rounded diet, however supplements can also be helpful. Periodically add specialist supplements to their food, like a powdered multivitamin. This makes it possible to guarantee that they get all the vital vitamins and minerals needed for optimum health.

11: Observing Consumption Patterns

Pay special attention to your hermit crab's eating patterns, as these might reveal a lot about their general health. Abrupt weight loss, changes in appetite, or a lack of interest in food could all be signs of a problem. Frequent monitoring enables you to identify possible health issues early on and take the necessary action.

12: Environmental Elements

The food requirements and appetite of your hermit crab can be affected by environmental factors. It is important to keep the habitat at the proper temperature and humidity levels because any deviations may affect the animals' metabolic processes and general health. Adapt feeding schedules and amounts to seasonal fluctuations or environmental shifts.

13: Things to Consider When Molting

Hermit crabs may display alterations in their dietary habits as they molt. Some could cut back on their intake or stop eating entirely. During this delicate period, honor their innate instincts and hold off on feeding them until they are back to their regular activities. It's important to stay well-hydrated when molting, so make sure there's always water nearby.

14: Tiny Dietary Adjustments

Abrupt dietary changes may cause hermit crabs to become sensitive. As you progressively introduce new foods, give them time to get used to the tastes and textures of them. This method reduces anxiety and guarantees that they will welcome new dishes to their menu.

15: Having a veterinarian consultation

Consult a veterinarian who specializes in exotic pets if you have questions concerning the food of your hermit crab or if you observe consistent alterations in its eating patterns. A specialist can offer advice that are specifically designed to meet the demands of your hermit crab, promoting their long-term health and wellbeing.

In conclusion, the health and happiness of your hermit crab greatly depend on a thoughtful and diverse diet. Through comprehension of their nutritional requirements, provision of a variety of high-quality foods, and accommodation of their specific inclinations, you augment the general welfare of these fascinating crustaceans, cultivating a prosperous and satisfying existence in confinement.

Chapter 3

Selecting the Correct Shells: An Understanding of the Process

A vital component of caring for hermit crabs is selecting the right shells, which affects not just their physical health but also their behavior and development. We will explore the nuances of shell selection in detail in this in-depth examination, offering insights into the habits of hermit crabs in their natural habitat and helping you select the appropriate shells for your crustacean friends.

1: The Importance of Shells in the Biology of Hermit Crabs
Among crustaceans, hermit crabs are distinct because they rely on external shells for protection. Hermit crabs have a soft, delicate abdomen in contrast to other crabs that have a hard exoskeleton. They look for and live

inside empty gastropod shells, like those of snails, in order to protect themselves. Selecting a suitable shell is essential for their survival, development, and general health.

2: Preference for Natural Shell

It's critical to comprehend hermit crabs' innate preferences about shells. Hermit crabs are picky about the kind, dimensions, and forms of the shells they prefer. They like shells that have a large hole so that they may fully withdraw their bodies inside for protection. Their selection is also influenced by the weight and curvature of the shell.

3: Expanding and Shifting Shells

Hermit crabs go through a process called molting, in which they lose their exoskeleton to make room for growth, therefore their size is never constant. They might need a bigger shell during molting to fit their expanding bodies. It is essential to provide them a range of shell options so when they outgrow their present one, they can quickly choose an appropriate replacement.

4: Providing a Range of Shell Choices

Provide your hermit crabs with a variety of shells that vary in size, shape, and aperture to meet their varied demands. Add turbos as well as murex shells, since hermit crabs tend to favor these. Every crab can select a shell that fits and suits their unique preferences by trying out several possibilities.

5: Examining and Choosing Shells

Hermit crabs choose out their new shells very carefully. They examine possible shells in great detail, typically trying a few before choosing the one that best fits their requirements. This behavior highlights how crucial it is to have a range of shells in the ecosystem to promote choice and exploration.

6: Behavior Shifting Shell

Hermit crabs naturally change their shells, and they do so for a variety of reasons. It could be brought on by maturation, the need for a safer or cozier shell, or even the effects of social interactions. Your hermit crab's comfort level and general well-being can be inferred from shell-changing behavior.

7: Stress's Function in Shell Alterations

Stress has a big impact on how hermit crabs alter their shells. Stress can be brought on by alterations in the surroundings, disruptions, or hostile tank companions, which makes a hermit crab search for a new shell. Maintaining a steady and comfortable environment reduces shell alterations brought on by stress.

8: Examining Shell Fit

A hermit crab's health depends on how well its shell fits. An overly tight or loose shell might obstruct eating, make it difficult to move, and add needless stress. Keep an eye on your hermit crabs to make sure their shells offer sufficient protection while facilitating easy mobility.

9: Upkeep of Shells

To guarantee that shells are suitable for hermit crabs, regular maintenance is required. Shells should be cleaned by removing any dirt, algae, or other impurities. Before reintroducing shells to their natural habitat, boiling them helps clean them and lowers the possibility of dangerous pathogens. Furthermore, repair any damaged shells and routinely check them for wear indicators.

10: Real versus Man-Made Shells

Although hermit crabs naturally prefer the shells of gastropods, some fans have tried giving their pets artificial shells made of ceramic or plastic materials.

Even though these might be more durable and require less upkeep, it's important to watch how hermit crabs react to artificial possibilities. While some might accept them with ease, others would prefer the comfort of real shells.

11: Shell Interactions and Social Dynamics

Social dynamics in a multi-hermit crab ecosystem can affect the choice of shell. The most attractive shells may be taken by dominant crabs, giving their subordinates less choices. A sufficient quantity of shells and social interaction monitoring reduce the likelihood of disputes over shell supply.

12: Ensuring Diversity of Shells in the Environment

There's more to keeping a habitat healthy than merely providing a variety of shells. Add fresh shells to the habitat on a regular basis to allow for exploration and possible improvements. This not only accommodates the hermit crabs' innate behavior but also makes sure they have access to growing shells.

13: Enrichment and Shell Stores

Adding items such as "shell shops," which are places within the habitat where extra shells are placed to encourage hermit crabs to explore and maybe change shells, is one way to create a dynamic and enriching ecosystem. They benefit from this enrichment activity in terms of brain stimulation and general wellbeing.

14: Dealing with Shell Disengagement

For a variety of causes, including discontent with the shell's fit or quality, hermit crabs may give up on their shells. Look into the possible causes of any abandoned shells you come across in the ecosystem. It can indicate stress, medical problems, or contact with other crabs.

15: Getting Expert Counsel

Advice from a veterinarian who specializes in exotic pets is crucial if you have trouble choosing a shell or see worrying behavior associated with shells. An expert can evaluate the circumstances, provide direction on shell selections, and take care of any underlying environmental or health problems.

To sum up, choosing the right shell is a complex part of caring for hermit crabs, affecting their general well-being, behavioral expression, and physical comfort. You can help ensure your hermit crab buddies have a happy and healthy existence by being aware of the natural behaviors related to shells, offering a variety of options, and keeping a careful eye on their relationships.

Chapter 4

Temperature and Humidity: Establishing the Perfect Setting

When taking care of hermit crabs, it's critical to maintain the proper temperature and humidity levels. Their development, general well-being, and capacity to exhibit natural behaviors all depend on these environmental elements. We will go into the nuances of controlling humidity and temperature in this in-depth investigation, helping you to provide the best possible habitat for your hermit crab friends.

1. Conditions of Natural Habitats

Prior to getting into the details of designing the perfect home, it's important to comprehend the natural environmental circumstances that hermit crabs prefer. Hermit crabs are found in tropical and subtropical locations; they live near coasts where they have access to both land and water. These areas usually see temperatures between 75 and 85°F (24 and 29°C), along with high humidity levels between 70 and 80%.

2: Managing the Habitat's Temperature

Hermit crab metabolism depends on maintaining a consistent temperature. Since they are ectothermic, the temperature of their surroundings affects their body temperature. Use an under-tank heater to create a cozy and warm environment. To create a heat gradient and enable hermit crabs to migrate between warmer and colder regions according to their inclinations, place it on one side of the tank.

3. How Important Thermoregulation Is

Hermit crabs control their body temperature through thermoregulation. They can self-regulate by choosing places in the ecosystem that best meet their demands when there is a heat gradient. This is in line with their natural tendency to warm up in the sun and then seek the shade to cool off.

4: Checking and Modifying the Temperature

Use a trustworthy thermometer to regularly check the habitat's temperature. As the indoor temperature fluctuates or the seasons change, make the necessary adjustments. Because hermit crabs are sensitive to abrupt changes in temperature and may become stressed or have health problems, avoid unexpected temperature extremes.

5. Complete Range Lighting

Hermit crabs benefit from full-spectrum lighting in addition to appropriate temperature maintenance. UVB rays from natural sunshine are vital for the production of vitamin D, which is required for calcium metabolism and general health. If it is not possible to have natural sunshine, replicate natural circumstances with UVB lights made specifically for reptiles.

6: Regulation of Humidity

For hermit crab health, achieving and sustaining the right humidity levels is equally important. Due to the modification of their gills, hermit crabs need a humid atmosphere in order to exchange gases effectively. Stress, trouble molting, and respiratory problems might result from low humidity. To increase humidity levels, spritz the habitat frequently with dechlorinated water. If you want to precisely measure humidity, think about using a hygrometer.

7: Supplying Dishes for Shallow Water

Incorporate shallow water dishes within the habitat to maintain humidity levels and to give people access to water for bathing and drinking. To avoid unintentional drowning, make sure the water is dechlorinated and maintain the appropriate depth. Through their gills, hermit crabs take in water, which they then utilize to maintain the humidity of their gill chambers, which aids in effective breathing.

8: Moisture Substratum

The moisture content of the substrate is a key factor in humidity maintenance. Select a moisture-retaining substrate, like a blend of sand, sphagnum moss, and coconut coir. Mist the substrate frequently to keep it from drying out, and keep an eye on the moisture content to maintain a continuously damp atmosphere.

9: Solubility and Melting

When molting, it's very important to be properly hydrated. Hermit crabs are particularly vulnerable during molting, when they lose their exoskeleton to make room for growth. Maintaining a humid climate facilitates molting and helps avoid problems like hard shedding or partial molts. To support their physiological needs during molting stages, maintain greater humidity levels.

10: Difficulties with Temperature and Humidity

Stability of the temperature and humidity in the hermit crab's habitat might be threatened by a number of circumstances. The inside environment can be impacted by external factors including heating, air conditioning, and weather variations. Maintain a stable microclimate by checking and adjusting the temperature and humidity settings on a regular basis to offset outside fluctuations.

11: Seasonal Modifications

Owners of hermit crabs should be aware of seasonal variations and modify the habitat as necessary. In order to keep a comfortable temperature throughout the winter months, extra heating could be required. On the other hand, during warmer months, it's important to keep an eye out for potential overheating and to offer cooling alternatives like covered spaces or more misting.

12: Airflow and Ventilation

Proper ventilation is just as vital to avoid mold growth and maintain air quality as maintaining high humidity levels. Make sure the habitat has enough airflow by using mesh screens or lids with good ventilation. Maintaining a balance between ventilation and humidity is essential to giving your hermit crabs a healthy habitat.

13: Tracking Conduct in Reaction to Circumstance

Crabs that live alone exhibit great environmental responsiveness. Keep a watchful eye on their behavior, as any changes may be a sign of unhappiness with the surroundings. Hermit crabs may be uncomfortable and may have problems with humidity or temperature if they regularly remain in one place or show signs of discomfort such as grooming with extended antennae.

14: Seasonal Modifications

Owners of hermit crabs should be aware of seasonal variations and modify the habitat as necessary. In order to keep a comfortable temperature throughout the winter months, extra heating could be required. On the other hand, during warmer months, it's important to keep an eye out for potential overheating and to offer cooling alternatives like covered spaces or more misting.

15: Getting Expert Counsel

Seeking guidance from a veterinarian with experience in exotic pets is advised if you have trouble keeping your hermit crabs at the ideal temperature and humidity or if you observe consistent behavioral changes in them. A specialist can evaluate the circumstances, offer direction on modifying the surroundings, and take care of any underlying medical issues or stress-related issues.

In summary, a careful balance between temperature and humidity regulation must be struck in order to create and preserve the perfect habitat for hermit crabs. You may support the general health, comfort, and well-being of these fascinating crustacean friends by being aware of their natural habitat circumstances, offering a variety of temperature alternatives, and making sure that the humidity level is constant.

Chapter 5

Taking Care of Your Hermit Crab and Getting Along with It: Appropriate Ways to

Hermit crabs are intriguing crustaceans, and handling and interacting with them requires a thorough approach that takes into account their specific qualities and activities. We will go over how to connect with your hermit crab in this in-depth guide, stressing the value of establishing a stress-free environment and encouraging good relationships.

1: Comprehending the Behavior of Hermit Crabs

It's crucial to comprehend hermit crab behavior in its native habitat before handling or interacting with these creatures. These animals are renowned for being timid and bashful. They seek cover from potential threats in their shells and depend on them for security in the wild.

Positive engagement is based on mutual understanding and appreciation for these actions.

2: Building Confidence

When dealing with hermit crabs, confidence must be earned gradually. Start off by letting them get used to their new surroundings before you handle them. Take the time to watch how they behave, take note of where they like to hide, and get to know their daily schedule. The foundation for a more laid-back and trustworthy relationship is laid by this patience.

3: Reducing Anxiety

Because hermit crabs are sensitive to environmental changes, unneeded stress can be harmful to their well-being. Reduce stressors by staying away from abrupt movements, loud noises, and habitat disruptions. Maintain a steady atmosphere with regular humidity and temperature levels to give people a feeling of security.

4: Identifying Stressful Symptoms

It's critical to recognize stress signals in hermit crabs. Anxiety can show up as frenetic movements, extended antennae, altered food habits, or other behaviors. If you see these symptoms, take another look at their surroundings to find and address any possible stresses.

5: Using Handfeeding to Foster Bonds

Hand feeding your hermit crab is a good method to interact with it. Serve finger food, bite-sized portions straight from your palm. This builds trust and lessens the fear people have of interacting with people by helping them link your presence with good things.

6: A Gradual Overview of Managing

You can start introducing handling to your hermit crab gradually after it appears at ease with you. To begin, put your hand softly in front of them without touching them directly. Let them investigate your hand at their own leisure. They can make contact and experience less stress thanks to this methodical technique.

7: The Cupping Method Use the cupping technique when you're ready to handle your hermit crab. Lift the hermit crab with one hand and let it land on your palm. Support its body gently with your other hand. Similar to the shelter their shells provide, cupping creates a safe, enclosed area. Steer clear of abrupt movements and remain composed at all times.

8: Delicate Handling Time
Handle sessions quickly, especially at the beginning. Extended handling might make hermit crabs feel threatened and stressed. You can progressively extend

the time as they get used to the interaction. Always keep an eye out for any indications of discomfort in their behavior, and if necessary, quickly return them to their habitat.

9: Dealing with Frequency

Hermit crabs don't need to be handled very often, and too much engagement can be stressful. Keep handling sessions to a few times per week so that they have enough time to recuperate and behave naturally. Keeping an eye on how they react to handling allows you to determine how comfortable they are with you and helps you plan future interactions.

10: Comprehending Sensitivity to Molting

Hermit crabs are particularly vulnerable when they are molting. Steer clear of dealing with them during this crucial period as any interruption may cause tension and possible issues. During molting, provide them a peaceful, uncluttered environment so they can finish this natural process unhindered.

11: Providing Opportunities for Climbing

Add climbing structures to improve the habitat of your hermit crab. Since hermit crabs are naturally inclined to climb, offering them opportunity to do so will replicate how they would behave in the wild. Climbing structures, such coconut hides or driftwood, encourage physical activity and a healthier, more active lifestyle.

12: Establishing a Secure Exploration Zone

Establish a secure location for supervised exploration outside the habitat. Here is a good spot to set up a small dish of dechlorinated water so your hermit crab may explore and play in the water. To guarantee their safety during these times of discovery, always keep a tight eye on them.

13: Presenting Tank Companions

Your hermit crab might benefit from having pals in the tank. Since they are gregarious animals, having other hermit crabs in the environment can be advantageous. But keep a close eye on how they interact to avoid hostility, and make sure there are many hiding places to ease tension.

14: Dealing with Aggressive Conduct

It's critical to act quickly if you notice any aggressive behaviors in hermit crabs, such as shell wrestling or extremely domineering behavior. Provide more places to hide, and if needed, think about confining hostile people in a makeshift isolation tank until their behavior calms down.

15: Creating a Connection by Observation

There's more to bonding with a hermit crab than just handling. Take time to observe their distinct personalities, inclinations, and habits. You will be in a better position to establish an environment that promotes their well-being the more you comprehend about their innate tendencies and reactions.

16: Getting Expert Counsel

Consult a veterinarian with experience with exotic pets if you are having trouble controlling your hermit crabs or if you observe consistent behavioral changes in them. A specialist can evaluate the circumstances, offer direction on social skills, and take care of any underlying medical issues or stress-related issues.

In summary, managing and engaging with hermit crabs necessitates tolerance, deference, and a thorough comprehension of their innate tendencies. You can help ensure these fascinating crustacean companions are happy and healthy by providing a stress-free environment, introducing handling gradually, and encouraging pleasant interactions.

Chapter 6

Health Indications: Recognizing and Treating Typical Hermit Crab Problems

You must take proactive measures and keep a close eye on your hermit crabs to ensure their health and wellbeing. This thorough tutorial will cover frequent problems that may occur while hermit crabs are in captivity, as well as the different health indicators you should be aware of in them.

1: Consistent Health Assessment

Setting up a schedule for frequent health checks is the first step in keeping your hermit crabs healthy. Observations of their behavior, eating patterns, and general look on a daily basis offer important clues about their state of health. Any changes from their typical behaviors could be a symptom of possible health problems.

2. Signs of Healthy Behavior

It's crucial to comprehend what hermit crabs consider to be healthy behavior in order to identify health issues early on. Hermit crabs in good health usually lead active lives, exploring, climbing, and grooming as part of their innate habits. They should also have a typical feeding schedule and show an interest in eating.

3. Stress-Related Symptoms

In captivity, stress is a prevalent problem that can take many different forms in hermit crabs. Agitated movements, expanded antennae, altered eating patterns, and extensive hiding are all indicators of stress. For their general well-being to be maintained, stressors like disruptions or environmental changes must be recognized and dealt with.

4. Unexplained Posture or Sluggishness

Lethargy or unusual body postures may be signs of a medical problem. A hermit crab may indicate an underlying issue if it habitually hides or acts listlessly. Keep an eye on their activity levels and look into it more if you observe a noticeable decline in mobility.

5: Modifications to Shell Appearance

An important sign of a hermit crab's health is the state of its shell. To be protected, a shell must be whole and kept in good condition. Anomalies including excessive wear, staining, or damage to the shell could indicate aggressive behavior, malnutrition, or problems with the shell.

6. Irregularities in Molting

Hermit crabs naturally undergo molting, which enables them to develop and regenerate their exoskeleton. However, there may be health hazards associated with molting process anomalies. Intervention may be required if a hermit crab exhibits symptoms of incomplete molting, has trouble shedding its exoskeleton, or struggles during the molting process.

7: Indices of Illness

Identifying symptoms of disease is essential for prompt treatment. Hermit crabs frequently experience health problems such as sluggishness, color changes, aberrant growths, or obvious anomalies on the exoskeleton. Any abrupt and obvious changes in appearance or behavior need to be looked into in great detail.

8. Respiratory Distress

Because hermit crabs have modified gills for breathing, respiratory distress can result from any problems impacting their capacity to breathe. respiration difficulties, extended antennae grooming, or an increased dependence on shallow water for respiration are indicative of respiratory issues. Maintaining the right humidity levels is crucial to avoiding respiratory problems.

9: Infections with Parasites

Hermit crabs are susceptible to parasitic infections, which can cause symptoms like lethargy, weight loss, altered appetite, or exoskeleton-visible parasites. Check your hermit crabs frequently for parasite symptoms, and if you think your pet may be infected, speak with a veterinarian who has experience treating unusual animals.

10: Appropriate Management Methods

For the sake of your hermit crabs' wellbeing, you must handle them carefully. Inadequate management can result in stress, which can alter behavior and perhaps cause health problems. To reduce the chance of harm or stress while handling, create a safe, enclosed zone by using the cupping technique.

11: Aggression and Tank Companions

There may be conflicts over dominance and violence in a multi-hermit crab habitat. Keep a close eye out for aggressive behaviors in their interactions, such as shell wrestling or overbearing conduct. Having plenty of hiding places and paying attention to social dynamics can assist avert violent confrontations.

12: A Well-Balanced Diet for Optimal Nutrition

The key to a healthy hermit crab diet is balance. A number of health problems, such as weakening exoskeletons and increased susceptibility to illnesses, can result from nutritional shortages. To guarantee a well-rounded diet, provide a range of meals, such as commercial hermit crab pellets, fresh fruits, vegetables, and protein sources.

13: Supplementing with Calcium

The health of a hermit crab's exoskeleton depends on calcium. A calcium shortage can result in soft shells, more susceptibility to damage during molting, and generalized health problems. Offer foods high in calcium, such as crushed eggshells, cuttlebone, or real coral, and, if necessary, think about supplementing with calcium.

14: Checking the Condition of the Tank

Keeping your tank in good shape is essential to avoiding health problems. Check and maintain the habitat's humidity and temperature on a regular basis. Make sure the substrate is sufficiently moist, wash the water dishes frequently, and keep an eye out for any indications of bacterial or mold growth.

15: Measures for Quarantine

Quarantine measures must be followed when adding additional hermit crabs to an established habitat or if you believe one crab is ill. To stop the potential spread of illness, isolate the afflicted person in a different tank. This enables more thorough observation and, if required, focused treatment.

16: Looking for Veterinary Attention

It is crucial that you seek veterinary care from a specialist with experience in treating exotic pets if you observe any chronic health problems, behavioral changes, or illness-related indicators. Veterinarians are qualified to do in-depth examinations, offer precise diagnosis, and suggest suitable treatments for health issues pertaining to hermit crabs.

17: Enhancement of the Environment

Enriching the environment is crucial to fostering the mental and physical health of hermit crabs. Provide possibilities for exploration, hiding places, and climbing structures. To encourage their natural habits, engage in activities like hand-feeding, providing fresh shells, and setting up an active habitat.

18: Identifying Mating Behavior Signs

It is crucial to identify signals of mating behavior in an environment with several hermit crabs. Courtship rituals, grooming exchanges, and even mating dances are examples of mating activities. By comprehending these actions, we can better prepare the environment so that prospective mating pairings can thrive.

19: Maintaining Records

It can be quite helpful to keep track of your hermit crab's behavior, eating habits, and any health issues that are noticed. Maintaining records enables you to monitor changes over time, spot trends, and give a veterinarian precise information should they need it.

20: Establishing a Molting-Friendly Environment

Hermit crabs are particularly susceptible during molting, so it's important to create a caring habitat. Maintain the right humidity levels, provide a range of shell alternatives, and try to keep molting times as disturbance-free as possible. A peaceful, safe setting is essential for a good molting process.

To sum up, proactive maintenance and routine health checks are essential to guaranteeing your hermit crabs' wellbeing. You may help ensure that these fascinating crustacean companions have a happy and healthy life by adopting appropriate care methods, identifying indications of stress or disease, and learning healthy behaviors. Always be aware of their requirements, get expert assistance when required, and provide a stimulating environment that promotes both their physical and emotional well-being.

Chapter 7

Molting Matters: Handling the Process of Molting Safely

For hermit crabs, molting is an essential and natural process that is vital to their growth, development, and general well-being. We will go over the specifics of the molting process, its importance to hermit crabs, and the precautions you need to take to make sure your crustacean friends are safe at this time.

1: Comprehending Hermit Crab Molting

Hermit crabs undergo a process called molting in order to remove their exoskeleton and make room for development. Hermit crabs are protected by their exoskeletons, unlike creatures with internal skeletons. The old exoskeleton sheds during the molting process and is replaced by a bigger one. Hermit crabs require molting in order to develop, repair exoskeleton damage, and regenerate amputated limbs.

2: Molting Frequency

Hermit crabs molt at different rates according to their age, species, and surroundings. Due to their rapid growth, young hermit crabs molt more regularly, whilst elderly animals may molt less frequently. Other variables that may affect the frequency of molting include temperature, humidity, and the availability of food.

3: Indications of Molting

Hermit crabs exhibit a number of symptoms prior to molting. These consist of behavioral adjustments including hiding more frequently, becoming less active, and losing weight. Furthermore, a hermit crab could seem restless and keep shifting around its home. It's critical to recognize these pre-molting indicators in order to provide the required support during this delicate time.

4: Establishing an Appropriate Molting Environment

Hermit crab health depends on providing an appropriate molting habitat. This entails keeping the habitat's temperature and humidity levels at appropriate levels. The substrate should have just enough moisture to make digging easier and provide the molting process the support it needs.

5. The Value of Humidity

An essential component of the molting process is humidity. Hermit crabs have unique gills that allow them to absorb moisture; hence, high humidity levels are essential to a successful molt. Insufficient humidity may make it harder for the exoskeleton to shed, which could cause problems or incomplete molts.

6: Considerations for Substrates

Choosing the right substrate is essential to establishing a molting-supportive habitat. A blend of sand, sphagnum moss, and coconut coir offers the perfect balance of structural support and moisture retention. In order to enable the hermit crab to bury itself during molting, the substrate needs to be sufficiently deep.

7: The Act of Molting

Hermit crabs have particular habits while they are molting. They start by excavating a tunnel in the substrate to provide a safe haven for molting. The hermit crab will assume a pre-molting posture when finishing its burrow, indicating the impending exoskeleton shedding.

8: Breaking Down the Exoskeleton

Ecdysis, the actual process by which the exoskeleton sheds, is a delicate and complex one. Enzymes secreted by the hermit crab facilitate the shedding of the old exoskeleton by softening it. After carefully removing its old exoskeleton, the crab leaves behind a new, delicate exoskeleton.

9: Care After Molting

Hermit crabs are especially delicate after molting and need extra attention. Over the course of several days, the new exoskeleton will gradually stiffen from its soft, malleable state. The hermit crab is more vulnerable to harm, predation, or hostility from other tank inhabitants at this time.

10: Providing a Calm and Noise-Free Ambience

It's important to have a calm, disturbance-free atmosphere both before and after molting. The molting hermit crab may become stressed and have a poor molting process if there are loud noises, abrupt movements, or disturbances. During this delicate period, minimize disruptions and refrain from handling or moving any things within the habitat.

11: Supplying Extra Shells

Hermit crabs may outgrow their present shells as they get larger. Make sure the habitat has an abundance of correctly sized shells to promote a successful molt. When molting, the hermit crab can select an appropriate replacement from a range of shell possibilities.

12: Keeping an eye out for issues

Even while molting is a normal process, issues might still occur. Having trouble removing the old exoskeleton entirely, having partial molts, or getting hurt during the molting process are common problems. Hermit crabs that are molting should be regularly inspected for any indications of problems, and you should be ready to step in if needed.

13: Handling Partially Completed Molts

When a hermit crab cannot completely shed its previous exoskeleton, incomplete molts take place. This may result in limb damage or mobility problems, among other health problems. Seek advice on possible actions from a veterinarian with experience treating exotic pets if you notice an incomplete molt.

14: Sustaining Hydration

Hermit crabs need to stay hydrated both during and after molting. Make sure the habitat has easy access to shallow dishes of dechlorinated freshwater. A molting hermit crab can find a place to hydrate and control its moisture levels in a water dish that is exceptionally deep.

15: Offering a Diet High in Calcium

For the development of a healthy exoskeleton, calcium is crucial. Providing a meal high in calcium, such as crushed eggshells, cuttlebone, and real coral, helps the hermit crab stay healthy overall and facilitates a successful molting process.

16: Identifying Post-Molt Patterns

Hermit crabs experience a period of recuperation following molting, during which they become more vulnerable. Reduced activity, increased concealment, and a transient decrease in hunger are examples of post-molt behaviors. The hermit crab can recuperate and strengthen its new exoskeleton by acknowledging and appreciating these activities.

17: Choosing a Shell After Molting

After molting, hermit crabs may select a new shell right away to fit their larger size. In the habitat, offer a range of shell choices, and pay attention to the hermit crab's choice of shell after it molts. This reduces the chance of vulnerability and guarantees they locate an appropriate shell quickly.

18: Preventing Unrest During the Hardening Process

The hardening of the exoskeleton of the hermit crab depends on the time after molting. Steer clear of disruptions during this stage since the soft exoskeleton is vulnerable to harm. Establish a steady, peaceful atmosphere so the hermit crab can finish hardening off without any disturbances.

19: Identifying Mating Patterns

Molting may occasionally be connected to mating activities. Hermit crabs can participate in grooming exchanges, courtship rituals, and, in some species, mating dances. By identifying these patterns of behavior, you can establish a conducive atmosphere for prospective mating partners.

20: Getting Expert Counsel

Consult a veterinarian with experience treating exotic pets if you run into difficulties or problems when your pet is molting. Expert advice may help with particular problems, offer remedies when needed, and guarantee your hermit crab's general health and wellbeing.

21: Maintaining Documents for Molting Cycles

It's helpful to keep track of your hermit crab's molting cycles in order to spot any anomalies and track patterns. Note the dates of molting, the behaviors that were seen during the process, and any issues or behavioral shifts that occurred afterwards. This material offers useful information for veterinary consultations and supports proactive treatment.

22: Taking Note of Organic Molting Cycles

Even while ideal conditions in captivity may cause hermit crabs to molt more frequently, it's crucial to watch their natural molting cycles. Steer clear of intentionally triggering molting as this can throw off their natural patterns and cause health issues. Hermit crabs are healthier when their molts occur in accordance with their natural cycles.

In conclusion, a key component of caring for hermit crabs is ensuring a healthy transition during molting. You help maintain the general health and vitality of your hermit crab pals by being aware of the warning indications of impending molting, setting up an appropriate molting environment, tending to them after molting, and identifying any potential difficulties. During this delicate time, always give priority to a peaceful, quiet environment. If necessary, seek professional assistance to address certain issues or difficulties.

Chapter 8

Social Dynamics: Perspectives on the Companionship and Behavior of Hermit Crabs

It is essential to comprehend the social dynamics of hermit crabs in order to give them the best care possible and establish a peaceful environment in captivity. We will examine the subtleties of hermit crab behavior, the value of company, and tips for maintaining a multi-hermit crab habitat in this in-depth investigation.

1. Hermit crabs are social creatures
Despite their name, hermit crabs are gregarious animals that frequently flourish in the company of other hermits. Hermit crabs typically inhabit groups in their natural habitat, known as colonies, which offer opportunities for prospective mating as well as social interaction.

Encouraging their well-being in captivity requires acknowledging and addressing their gregarious nature.

2. Advantages of Friendship

Hermit crabs that live together have many advantages, such as lower stress levels, higher activity levels, and chances to engage in socializing and grooming—two of their natural behaviors. Hermit crabs display a greater variety of behaviors in a communal setting, which creates a more lively and interesting atmosphere.

3. Innate Order and Hostility

Within their groups, hermit crabs create social hierarchies that may entail subdued interactions and demonstrations of power. Although most of the time these hierarchies are peaceful, there is the potential for occasional conflict, especially when vying for resources or between crabs of various sizes. It is essential to comprehend these dynamics in order to maintain a harmonious habitat.

4: Tank Dimensions and Design

Tank size and arrangement must be carefully considered in order to provide a space that encourages social interactions. For hermit crabs, a larger tank with lots of hiding places, climbing frames, and shells creates a more organic and lively environment. They can set up territories, explore, and communicate with one another much like they would in the wild thanks to this configuration.

5: Presenting the New Hermit Crabs

When adding new hermit crabs to an established colony, caution and gradual introduction are necessary. At first, place the new crab in a different section of the tank so the other crabs can get used to seeing it. To guarantee a seamless integration and stop any potential hostility, keep a tight eye on interactions.

6: Indices of Sympathy

Assessing the success of group dynamics requires looking for indications of compatibility between hermit crabs. Complementary crabs groom each other, share hiding places amicably, and adopt easy poses while they are together. Aggression or signs of stress could be indicators of compatibility problems that need to be addressed.

7: Keeping an eye on Shell Modifications

Hermit crabs trade shells frequently, a habit associated with their search for a cozy and suitable dwelling. Keeping an eye on shell modifications can reveal information about the social dynamics inside the community. To suit their preferences, make sure a range of shell selections are available. Also, keep an eye on interactions during shell exchanges.

8: Behaviors Related to Mating

Hermit crabs can participate in courtship rituals, grooming activities, and, in some cases, complex mating dances when they are in a communal environment. It is essential to identify these actions in order to comprehend the reproductive dynamics within the group and to establish a conducive environment for prospective mating partners.

9: Providing Sufficient Food

Hermit crabs depend on proper nourishment to sustain communal harmony. Make sure your diet is varied and well-balanced, including fresh produce, fruits, and vegetables as well as protein sources and commercial hermit crab pellets. Providing for their nutritional needs promotes group health overall and lessens rivalry for resources.

10: Activities for Social Enrichment

Hermit crabs benefit from social enrichment activities because they create a stimulating environment. Provide stuff for exploration, hiding places, and climbing structures. Furthermore, pleasant connections are made possible by hand-feeding hermit crabs since their association with people' positive experiences creates a more favorable social milieu.

11: Having Several Water Dishes Available

Water dishes should be provided in multiples for a multi-hermit crab environment. This guarantees that freshwater for bathing and drinking is readily available to all crabs. Having many water sources also lessens stress levels and the chance of competition within the group.

12: Identifying Stressful Symptoms

It's critical to keep an eye out for stress indicators in a social setting. A person experiencing stress may exhibit a variety of behaviors, such as agitated movements, altered eating patterns, or prolonged antennae grooming. Quickly addressing stressors—like adding more hiding places or modifying the surroundings—helps preserve a positive social dynamic.

13: Compatibility with Shell

Maintaining shell compatibility is essential to reducing intragroup disputes. Hermit crabs have been known to wrestle with their shells or try to grab another crab's via force. Offering a variety of shell forms and sizes lessens rivalry and enables every crab to locate a good home without acting aggressively.

14: Dealing with Aggressive Conduct

Hermit crabs are normally calm creatures, but they can become aggressive when they meet new people or when they are vying for the same resources. In order to address aggressive behavior, more hiding places should be provided, interactions should be thoroughly observed, and, if required, aggressive people should be temporarily isolated to reduce tension.

15: Providing Sufficient Hiding Places

Sufficient hiding places are necessary to reduce stress and give hermit crabs the freedom to hide when necessary. Make sure the tank is filled with enough hiding places, such caves, driftwood, and coconut hides. This enables every crab to mark its territory and withdraw during molting or socializing periods.

16: Molting and Shell Changes

Hermit crabs are especially vulnerable during molting, and disputes over shells might occur. During molting periods, give extra shells to help alleviate potential problems. Furthermore, keep a tight eye on interactions and step in to stop aggressive behaviors that can harm molting hermit crabs.

17: Group Dynamics: Size Considerations

Group dynamics are influenced by size, so larger hermit crabs may display dominance over smaller ones. Offering a range of shell sizes makes it easier to meet the group's various needs. In order to avoid size-based competition, make sure there are adequate resources, such as food and hiding places.

18: Establishing an Energetic Setting

Preventing boredom and fostering social connections require a lively atmosphere. Add components such as climbing frames, exploratory toys, and new habitat additions. These characteristics promote organic behaviors and support a lively and interesting social setting.

19: Hygiene and Tank Maintenance

In a social gathering, tension and illness can be avoided by keeping the tank clean and sanitary. Keep an eye on substrate conditions, clean water dishes on a regular basis, and remove any uneaten food. The general health of the hermit crab population is enhanced by a clean environment, which lowers the possibility of bacterial or fungal development.

20: Getting Expert Counsel

It's best to consult a veterinarian with experience in exotic pets if you have trouble handling the social dynamics of hermit crabs or notice ongoing aggression. A expert can evaluate the circumstances, offer direction on handling social concerns, and guarantee each member of the group is safe.

21: Maintaining Documents for Social Observations

It is helpful to keep note of social interactions and observations in order to spot patterns and recognize any behavioral shifts. Maintaining records enables you to keep an eye on social dynamics, identify personal preferences, and supply precise information in the event that expert advice is requested.

22: Acknowledging Social Changes and Aging

Hermit crabs' social dynamics can alter as they get older. Elderly people may become less socially active or favor solitary activities. Acknowledging these modifications enables habitat modifications arrangement, offering more places to hide or granting more personal space when required.

In summary, an essential component of proper care is comprehending and regulating the social dynamics of hermit crabs. Through acknowledging their social character, creating an environment that suits them, and resolving any disagreements, you help to ensure the happiness and well-being of these fascinating crustacean friends. To maintain a peaceful and prosperous hermit crab community, make sure the habitat suits their social needs, constantly monitor their behavior, and, when needed, consult an expert.

chapter 9

Tank Upkeep: Maintaining a Scenic and Cozy Habitat

Hermit crabs require a clean, cozy habitat to be maintained for their health and welfare. We will go over many areas of tank maintenance in this comprehensive guide, including as cleaning techniques, substrate care, water quality control, and establishing an environment that encourages the natural activities of these interesting crustaceans.

1. The Value of Tank Upkeep

Maintaining your aquarium in a way that closely resembles the natural habitat of hermit crabs is essential. Stress levels are lowered, disease risks are decreased, and optimal health is promoted by a clean and well-maintained tank. Hermit crabs can show their natural habits and flourish in captivity when proper upkeep is provided.

2: Supportive Care

The substrate, which provides the groundwork for digging, burrowing, and molting, is an essential part of the habitat for hermit crabs. To keep the ideal substrate conditions:

Depth: Make sure that the substrate is at least 6 inches deep. Hermit crabs feel secure since they can carry out their normal activities, such as burrowing and excavating, at this depth.

Moisture: Regular misting will help to maintain the substrate's moisture content. Because hermit crabs have unique gills that allow them to absorb water, molting requires the right amount of moisture. Use dechlorinated water to stay away from dangerous substances.

Use a substrate mix consisting of sand, sphagnum moss, and coconut coir. For hermit crab activities, this combination offers the ideal texture, moisture retention, and structure.

3: Hiding Spot Sanitation

Hideouts are essential to hermit crab security and stress relief. Maintain these spaces tidy to stop bacteria and garbage from building up. Driftwood, coconut skins, and other constructions should be routinely inspected and cleaned as needed. Make sure that hiding places are kept clear of food scraps and debris.

4. Handling Water Quality

Hermit crabs require clean, dechlorinated water to be maintained for their welfare. To manage the quality of your water, abide by following guidelines:

Water Dishes: Offer bathing and drinking glasses with shallow water. To guarantee a steady supply of clean water, clean these dishes on a regular basis and refill them with dechlorinated water.

Saltwater Baths: Periodic saltwater baths are beneficial for hermit crabs as well. To make a saltwater bath solution, use marine aquarium salt. This promotes the health of their exoskeleton and osmoregulation.

Water Quality Testing: Check the quality of the water on a regular basis, particularly if you use tap water. Monitoring tools are useful for keeping an eye on things like pH, ammonia, nitrite, and nitrate levels. Make sure these are within the range that hermit crabs can tolerate.

5: Sanitizing and Cleaning

In order to keep things sanitary and stop dangerous bacteria from growing, the tank's components should be cleaned and sanitized on a regular basis:

Substrate Sifting: To get rid of waste, molting exoskeletons, and uneaten food, periodically sift through the substrate. By doing this, unpleasant smells are avoided and the substrate used by hermit crabs is kept clean.

Cleaning Decorations: Give artificial plants, driftwood, and pebbles in your tank a thorough rinse to make them clean. Hermit crabs may be harmed by chemical cleaning residues, so stay away from using them.

Cleaning of Water Dishes: To stop bacterial growth, wash water dishes frequently. Before replenishing with new, dechlorinated water, give the dishes a thorough cleaning with a gentle brush.

Examine the shells in the habitat on a regular basis. Provide a range of clean shells for the hermit crabs to select from, and remove any damaged or contaminated ones.

6: Steer clear of dangerous substances

Hermit crabs are delicate to substances and chemicals that may be hazardous to their well-being. Take the following preventative measures to keep dangerous materials out of the habitat:

Steer clear of pesticides: Make sure that no toxic chemicals or pesticides are present in any substrate or materials that are introduced to the habitat. Hermit crabs may be poisoned by pesticides.

Chlorinate Water: For misting, water dishes, and saltwater baths, use dechlorinated water. Hermit crabs may suffer injury from tap water containing chlorine and chloramines.

Safe Cleaning Supplies: Use safe, hermit crab-friendly cleaning supplies if you must clean. To avoid residue, make sure that all cleaning agents are completely washed.

7: Keeping Adequate Humidity Levels

Hermit crabs need a certain amount of humidity to maintain both their general health and ability to breathe. To keep the right level of humidity, adhere to these guidelines:

Misting Schedule: Create a misting schedule to keep the habitat's humidity levels stable. Make sure the substrate is sufficiently moist but avoid flooding it by using a thin mist.

Substrate Moisture: Consistently check the substrate's moisture content. Based on the moisture content of the substrate and the surrounding conditions, adjust the frequency of misting.

Humidity Gauges: To measure and track the amount of humidity, use a humidity gauge. To make sure the habitat's humidity level is constant throughout, place gauges in various locations throughout the tank.

8: Stopping Bacterial and Mold Growth

It takes a clean environment to stop mold and dangerous bacteria from growing. Put these precautions into action to reduce the risk:

Eliminate Uneaten Food: Immediately empty the tank of any uneaten food. Food that has decomposed can attract mold and germs, which can compromise the habitat's general cleanliness.

Good Ventilation: Make sure the tank has enough ventilation. Static environments that encourage the growth of mold can be avoided with good ventilation. Proper tank design or the use of mesh lids can help provide ventilation.

Inspection of the Substrate: Frequently check the substrate for mold growth. Remove the contaminated substrate and replace it with a new substrate mix if mold is found.

9: Supplying Sufficient Lighting

Despite the fact that hermit crabs are generally nocturnal, sustaining a normal day-night cycle in their habitat depends on having enough lighting:

Natural Lighting: Place the tank where it gets enough of natural light, but keep it out of direct sunlight since this might cause overheating. Hermit crabs' circadian cycle is aided by natural light.

Artificial Lighting: To replicate the cycle of day and night, use artificial lighting. Hermit crabs can benefit from a regular lighting schedule that can be established with time-controlled LED lights.

10: Checking the Temperature of the Tank

Hermit crab health and activity depend heavily on maintaining proper temperatures. Adhere to these recommendations for temperature control:

Temperature Range: Maintain the tank's temperature between 75°F and 85°F (24°C and 29°C), which is the ideal range for hermit crabs. To consistently check temperatures, use a thermometer.

Heating devices: To keep temperatures steady, employ heating devices like under-tank heaters as needed. To avoid overheating, make sure that heat sources are appropriately managed.

Cooling Measures: If necessary, take cooling measures throughout the warmer months. This can involve putting frozen objects—like frozen water bottles—in the tank to reduce temperature and turning on fans to increase airflow.

11: Examining the Conduct of Hermit Crabs

Monitoring hermit crab activity on a regular basis is an important part of tank upkeep. Observe their relationships, activities, and any indications of illness or suffering. Early problem identification enables timely action and habitat condition modifications.

12: Measures for Quarantine

It is imperative to follow quarantine protocols while acclimating newly acquired hermit crabs to an established environment. Before reintroducing them to the main habitat, observe newly arrived individuals in a separate tank. This enables more thorough observation of the recent additions and aids in the containment of possible illnesses.

13: Maintaining Documents

It is advantageous to keep track of tank conditions, maintenance tasks, and any noted behavioral changes in hermit crabs. Maintaining records serves as a guide for monitoring trends, spotting any problems, and easing consultation with a veterinarian in the event that expert guidance is required.

14: Activities for Enrichment

For hermit crabs, enrichment activities are beneficial to their general health. Give people things to climb, explore, and engage with. New shells or intriguing structures are examples of novel habitat improvements that encourage natural activities and keep them from becoming bored.

15: Getting Expert Counsel

If you have trouble keeping the habitat in good condition or notice recurring problems, consult a veterinarian with experience treating exotic animals. Seeking expert advice can help with problem diagnosis, offering suitable solutions, and guaranteeing your hermit crabs' long-term wellbeing.

16: Establishing a Cozy Molting Setting

Hermit crabs are particularly vulnerable during molting, so make sure their surroundings are cozy during this time. Make sure the substrate is sufficiently moist, supply more shells, and keep disruptions to a minimum. Establishing a calm and safe environment facilitates a successful molt.

17: Handling Modifications in Behavior

Look into possible stressors or health problems if you see noticeable behavioral changes in hermit crabs, such as tiredness, changes in eating, or odd hiding. Taking quick action to address behavioral changes helps create a cozy and happy living space.

18: Frequent Medical Exams

Examine your hermit crabs' health on a regular basis to spot any anomalies or symptoms of sickness. Examine their overall look, shell condition, and exoskeleton.

Timely action and appropriate care are made possible by early recognition of health concerns.

19: Adapting Habitats for Senior Citizens

Hermit crabs' requirements may vary as they become older. Think about making the habitat more suited for elderly people, adding more hiding places, or designing a layout that suits their tastes. Hermit crabs that are getting older benefit from having their requirements recognized and met, which enhances their comfort and overall wellbeing.

20: Arranging for Shell Modifications

As a way to prepare for and anticipate shell changes, keep a range of clean, suitably sized shells on hand. Examine the habitat's shells on a regular basis and offer fresh choices to suit the tastes of hermit crabs going through shell changes.

In conclusion, hermit crab health depends critically on keeping their habitat tidy and cozy. You may establish an atmosphere where these intriguing crustaceans can flourish by taking good care of the substrate, the water quality, the cleaning techniques, and the overall circumstances of the surrounding area. Maintaining documentation, keeping an eye on things, and getting expert help when necessary all help ensure your hermit crab friends are happy and healthy in the long run.

Chapter 10

Being Prepared for Unexpected Events: Emergency Preparedness

Being ready for emergencies is essential to responsible hermit crab ownership, as it guarantees the safety and survival of these interesting crabs in unanticipated circumstances. We will go over the essential elements of hermit crab emergency planning in this extensive guide, including health emergencies, habitat problems, evacuation strategies, and veterinary professional communication.

1: Realizing the Value of Being Ready for Emergencies

Being ready for emergencies means preparing ahead of time and allocating resources to deal with unforeseen circumstances. Being prepared for unexpected crises and having the equipment and know-how to handle them quickly are important for owners of hermit crabs. You can reduce dangers and give your hermit crab friends prompt attention by creating a strong emergency plan.

2. Readiness for Health Emergencies

2.1: Identifying Symptoms of Illness

The first line of defense against a health emergency is knowing when hermit crabs become ill. Lethargy, changes in hunger, anomalies in the appearance of the exoskeleton, and strange behaviors are typical indicators of disease. Frequent observation enables you to recognize early sickness symptoms and respond quickly.

2.2: Assembling a First Help Package

Putting together a first aid kit for hermit crabs is crucial to taking care of minor medical emergencies quickly. The kit ought to have things like:

A distinct container designated for the isolation of ill or injured hermit crabs.

Dechlorinated Water: To wash, take a bath, and stay hydrated.

Hermit Crab-Safe Antibiotic Ointment: For small cuts or abrasions on shells.

Extra Shells: Keeping extra shells on hand in case of emergencies involving molting shells.

Soft Brush: To remove debris and clean shells gently.

2.3: Setting Up a Protocol for Quarantine

When a hermit crab becomes ill or when you introduce new ones, you must follow a quarantine regimen. In order to stop any potential infections from spreading, isolate the afflicted crab in a different tank. Keep a close eye on the person in quarantine and consult a veterinarian if symptoms intensify or persist.

3. Emergency Preparedness for Habitats

3.1: Recognizing Possible Problems with the Habitat

Being aware of possible habitat problems is essential for emergency readiness. Problems with the substrate, variations in temperature, problems with the quality of the water, and device failures are common habitat challenges. Evaluate the habitat on a regular basis in order to spot possible problems early on and take appropriate action.

3.2: Substitute Replacement in an Emergency

It's important to be ready to replace the substrate quickly if it gets polluted, moldy, or offers a health danger. Store enough pre-moistened substrate that is safe for hermit crabs on hand to replace the old substrate in a timely and secure manner. This guarantees the hermit crabs a hygienic and comfortable habitat.

3.3: Standby Lighting and Heating

Having backup heating and lighting options is crucial in case of a power outage or equipment malfunction. Battery-powered LED lights offer temporary illumination until power is restored, while heat pads or other alternate heat sources can help maintain appropriate temperatures. Always check the functionality of backup devices on a regular basis.

3.4: Emergency Procedures for Water Quality

Hermit crab health depends on promptly addressing acute problems with water quality. Use dechlorinated water for emergency water changes if there are any worries about the quality of the water. When chronic problems arise, carefully monitor the water's properties and get expert assistance.

4: Planning for Evacuations

4.1: Formulating an Evacuation Strategy

When you have to temporarily relocate your hermit crabs, it's imperative that you prepare for an evacuation. Create a thorough evacuation strategy that consists of:

shipping Containers: Prepare appropriate shipping containers in advance, such as airtight plastic containers or safe carriers.

Emergency Supplies: Bring necessary supplies, like as extra substrate, water dishes, shells, and a tiny amount of their familiar habitat.

Travel Heat Source: To keep cargo at the right temperature while in transit.

4.2: Locating Secure Areas

Decide on secure areas to temporarily move your hermit crabs in case of an evacuation. Take into account the surrounding environment, accessibility, and the availability of required materials. A friend's house, a family member's residence, or an emergency shelter are examples of safe places.

4.3: Sharing Plans for Evacuation

Share your evacuation preparations with family members and anyone who may be in charge of your hermit crabs' care. Make sure everyone is aware of the evacuation protocols, where the emergency supplies are located, and how crucial it is to relocate quickly and safely.

5. Interaction with Veterinary Experts

5.1: Building a Bond with a Veterinarian Who Lives in a Hermit Crab

One of the most important aspects of disaster planning is early and proactive consultation with a veterinarian skilled in hermit crab care. Before any emergencies arise, establish a relationship with a certified veterinarian. Tell them about your hermit crabs' living conditions, habitat, and any current health issues.

5.2: Contact Details for Emergencies

Keep a list of the emergency contact details for your veterinarian and nearby animal emergency clinics for your hermit crab. Provide their addresses, phone numbers, and any special instructions on how to get in touch with them in an emergency.

5.3: Options for Telehealth

Speak with your veterinarian about telehealth options for hermit crabs. In certain circumstances, it may be possible to have a remote consultation in which you can ask questions and receive answers without having to go to the clinic. Learn the procedure and make sure you have the equipment needed for online consultations.

6: Maintaining Records

6.1: Keeping Up Medical Records

Having accurate records on hand is a great way to be ready for emergencies. Maintain thorough health records for every hermit crab you know about, including details on shell changes, molting cycles, behavioral observations, and any medical interventions or treatments. In an emergency, this information helps veterinary specialists by giving them precise specifics.

6.2: Recording Conditions of the Habitat

Recording the state of the habitat is also crucial. Note any modifications you make to the substrate, equipment upkeep, humidity and temperature, and other aspects of the habitat. In addition to offering a thorough history of the ecosystem, these records help identify possible problems in case of emergency.

7: Resources and Community Support

7.1: Engaging with Communities of Hermit Crabs

Participating in forums and communities for hermit crabs offers helpful resources and assistance. Interact with knowledgeable hermit crab keepers, impart knowledge, and ask for help when required. Having a network of informed people to call in an emergency might be quite helpful.

7.2: Guides and Online Resources

To find out more about taking care of hermit crabs and being prepared for emergencies, consult internet resources and instructions. Keep up with the most recent advancements, scientific discoveries, and neighborhood conversations. During an emergency, trustworthy websites, care manuals, and online forums can be very helpful sources of information.

8. Frequent Exercises and Training

8.1: Carrying Out Emergency Exercises

Practice emergency exercises on a regular basis to make sure you and your family members understand how to handle transport containers, establish temporary habitats, and evacuate. To improve readiness, rehearse handling typical crises such substrate replacement or abrupt temperature changes.

8.2: Emergency First Aid Certification

Assemble the information and abilities required for providing emergency first aid. Discover how to handle small wounds, problems with shells, and other typical health issues. Veterinarian consultations, online courses, and manuals can offer important insights on emergency first aid for hermit crabs.

9: Adjusting to Modifying Circumstances

9.1: Keeping an Eye on Environmental Shifts

Keep up with changes in the environment that might have an impact on the habitat of your hermit crab. Keep abreast of any changes to the weather, possible power outages, and other issues that might affect their wellbeing. Being proactive in adjusting to circumstances guarantees that you are able to react quickly to new circumstances.

9.2: Modifying Emergency Protocols

Review and update your emergency preparations on a regular basis to reflect any changes to your living arrangements, the quantity of hermit crabs you possess, or habitat adjustments. Making necessary changes to emergency plans keeps them current and functional in dealing with changing situations.

10: Wrap-up

To sum up, emergency readiness is a thorough and continuous commitment to your hermit crab friends' welfare. You can build a robust framework for handling unforeseen circumstances by being aware of health emergencies, taking care of possible habitat problems, creating evacuation plans, encouraging communication with veterinary professionals, keeping records, looking for community support, and participating in regular training. For the long term health and well-being of your hermit crab friends, proactive preparation and prompt action in times of need are essential.

FAQs

1. What nourish hermit crabs?

In addition to commercial hermit crab chow, fresh fruits and vegetables, and protein sources like fish and mealworms, hermit crabs enjoy a varied diet. A varied and well-balanced diet is crucial to meet their nutritional needs.

2. How frequently should the substrate in the tank be changed?

To what extent a substrate changes depends on various aspects, including general condition, mold growth, and cleanliness. In general, it's best to swap out a section of the substrate every few months and, if needed, to replace the entire substrate.

3. Do solitary crabs require company?

Indeed, hermit crabs are gregarious animals that frequently flourish in the presence of other hermit crabs. It is advised to keep them in groups in order to encourage natural behaviors and lessen tension.

4. How can I provide my hermit crab with a suitable molting habitat?

Answer: Provide enough substrate depth for burrowing, maintain a calm and disturbance-free atmosphere, make sure the humidity levels are appropriate, and provide spare shells. A safe molting process is supported by these circumstances.

5. What is the ideal range of temperatures for hermit crabs?

Maintain a temperature range of 75°F to 85°F (24°C to 29°C) for the tank. Hermit crabs can become stressed by temperature changes, so use a thermometer to check and maintain a steady temperature.

6. Hermit crabs molt how often?

The frequency of hermit crabs' recurrent molting varies during their lifespan. It is a natural occurrence for them to lose their exoskeleton in order to grow. Molts may occur more frequently in younger crabs than in older ones.

7. Why do solitary crabs shed their shells?

Hermit crabs adapt their shells to fit their expanding bodies, is the answer. It's an essential behavior to their health. It's important to provide them a selection of tidy, suitable-sized shells to pick from.

8. If my hermit crab is sluggish or not eating, what should I do?

Answer: Loss of appetite and lethargy may indicate illness or stress. Verify the habitat, make sure the crabs are getting enough food, and think about scheduling a comprehensive examination with a veterinarian who specializes in caring for hermit crabs.

9. Can hermit crabs and other pets coexist in the same tank?

The ideal setting for hermit crabs is one without any other pets. Hermit crabs can be threatened by certain animals, and having other pets around can make them uncomfortable.

10. What are the signs that my hermit crab is molting?

Answer: Burying themselves in the substrate, less activity, and an appearance of a hazy exoskeleton are symptoms of molting. It's critical to create a peaceful environment and keep them from being disturbed as they molt.

Recall that individual hermit crab care may differ from what is indicated by these broad recommendations. Always keep a tight eye on your hermit crabs, and seek veterinary advice for any particular problems.

Made in the USA
Monee, IL
24 August 2024